AC Elec

Classes 86, 87, 90 and DVTs

MARK V. PIKE

KEY
Books

BRITAIN'S RAILWAYS SERIES, VOLUME 59

Front cover image: For many years this was a regular sight at London Euston. 87026 *Sir Richard Arkwright* (formerly *Redgauntlet*) and 87013 *John O' Gaunt* wait side by side for departure with expresses bound for the North. Which one would you have gone for? 26 May 1993.

Title page image: On display at Crewe Works open day is pioneer 87001 (formerly *Royal Scot* and *Stephenson*), returned to its original rail blue livery. The loco has since been preserved at the National Railway Museum. 31 May 2003.

Contents page image: 90044+90046 stand at Ipswich, awaiting the signal to proceed to the sidings with a Freightliner service. 27 September 2023.

Back cover image: The only example ever to carry Network Southeast livery in service, 86401 is immaculate on display at the Basingstoke rail fair. 26 September 1987.

Published by Key Books
An imprint of Key Publishing Ltd
PO Box 100
Stamford
Lincs PE9 1XQ

www.keypublishing.com

The right of Mark V. Pike to be identified as the author of this book has been asserted in accordance with the Copyright, Designs and Patents Act 1988 Sections 77 and 78.

Copyright © Mark V. Pike, 2024

ISBN 978 1 80282 825 2

Typeset by SJmagic DESIGN SERVICES, India.

Contents

Introduction

The Class 86 is an electric locomotive built during the mid-1960s. It was regarded at the time as an improvement on earlier Class 81–85s, which were really prototype locos. 100 Class 86s were built from 1965 to 1966, primarily to work passenger and freight trains on the newly electrified West Coast Main Line (WCML) from London Euston to various destinations including Birmingham, Crewe, Liverpool, Manchester and, later still, on to Glasgow. The introduction of these locos, alongside a handful of the Class 81–85s, thus enabled British Rail to withdraw large numbers of steam locomotives, with the last going during 1968.

The Class 87 was a development of the Class 86 and, from 1973, bolstered the existing electric traction fleet as well as furnishing service expansion. Rated at 5,000hp, these also fulfilled a requirement for a higher-performance electric locomotive compared to the Class 86's 3,600–4,040hp. The Class 87s became the prime electric locomotive for mainly passenger services until the late 1980s.

From the late 1980s there was another development. Originally classed as 87/2, the Class 90 was another 5,000hp machine. These locos were used for both passenger services and freight trains, and have served with various post-privatisation operators over the years, including Greater Anglia and Virgin Trains. However, they were withdrawn from regular passenger services during the late 2000s and 2010s, after being replaced by various electric units. The class does, however, remain in use on heavy freight trains operated by Freightliner, often in pairs, and examples are occasionally seen working charter services. Even so, freight company DBC has recently (2023) stopped using them.

All of the AC electrics have had long and relatively trouble-free careers, with a few members having now seen active service in the UK for almost 60 years. Some of the Class 86s remained in use on freight work with Freightliner until as recently as 2021. Also, a number of the Class 86s and 87s were exported

to Bulgaria and Hungary and remain in use today. Perhaps with the recent offer of DB Class 90s for sale, we will see some of these working abroad too. Most of these AC locos never seemed to garner quite as much interest as some other types of loco in the UK, but there is no denying that they have all provided some pretty solid service.

This is 90128 *Vrachtverbinding* on display in Exeter Riverside Yard during the Exeter rail fair. 5 May 1994.

Chapter 1

Class 86

Starting off this volume is one of my earliest shots of a Class 86 at the iconic location of Crewe station. The driver is strolling up to board BR blue 86210 *City of Edinburgh*, waiting to depart south with a train for London Euston. Look at all those BRUTEs (British Rail Universal Trolley Equipment), now long since vanished from today's railway scene. This loco later went on to become 86902 but was scrapped during 2011, although I believe one cab has been preserved. 9 August 1985.

On the same day, we see 86429 *The Times* being assisted by 47538 as they wait to depart with a service for Liverpool. The overhead wires were de-energised somewhere between Crewe and Liverpool for planned works during this time, hence the need for the diesel pilot. The Class 86 was one of the locos (along with 86211 *City of Milton Keynes*) involved in a serious accident at Colwich Junction in September 1986, which resulted in both locos being scrapped. 9 August 1985.

Staying at Crewe for a short series of shots taken on the same day, we now see 86102 *Robert A Riddles* about to head north with a service from London Euston, carrying the familiar original style of Inter-City livery of the late 1980s/early 1990s. This loco was scrapped during April 2002. 7 April 1993.

At the same spot, 86252 *The Liverpool Daily Post* is in the revised form of Inter-City livery, and also about to head north with a train from London Euston. This loco was scrapped in August 2002. 7 April 1993.

Next up is 86240 *Bishop Eric Treacy*, speeding through the down main line with another express from London Euston for the north. Nowadays most (if not all) passenger services stop here. The loco was scrapped in April 2005. 7 April 1993.

Crewe was not all about passenger trains, of course. This is 86425 in Rail Express Systems (RES) livery, waiting to head south from the station with a parcels service. This loco was scrapped in January 2005. 7 April 1993.

It was a regular occurrence in this period for so-called dedicated locos to get a little muddled and pushed into use on other services. This was the case here as Railfreight Distribution-liveried 86428 *Aldaniti* is seen waiting to head south with a cross-country service' which it would have worked to either Birmingham New Street or Coventry, from where a diesel loco would take over. This loco went on to work with Freightliner (as 86628) and is one of a few that have recently been exported to Bulgaria in 2023 for further use. 7 April 1993.

For many years, the nearby Crewe Works held very popular public open days, which were a great opportunity to see various locos undergoing maintenance and sometimes actually under construction. This is the unique 86501, at the time operated by Freightliner, in works for maintenance. Incidentally, the loco can clearly be seen sporting a covered nameplate, but it turned out that it was fitted with *Crewe Basford Hall* plates in error. The previous loco to carry these plates had been a Class 90, later operated by EWS, and they were actually EWS property! They were therefore hastily removed from this Freightliner-operated engine, which thus remained nameless. This loco had been converted out of 86608 in 2000 (which involved re-gearing), but in March 2016, it was converted back to its earlier specification and resumed its former identity as 86608. However, it was exported to Bulgaria in 2023 for further use. 20 May 2001.

We now move to Birmingham New Street, where we see 86103 *Andre Chapelon* waiting in the gloom of the station with a service for London Euston. 22 April 1992.

Peeping out from that same gloom is 86206 *City of Stoke-on-Trent*. At some point, this loco has received a bit of a dent above the front centre windscreen. It was scrapped in February 2004. 22 April 1992.

Virgin Trains red-liveried 86242 *James Kennedy GC* is captured arriving with a train from London Euston. This loco was exported to Hungary in 2013. 17 July 1999.

Also arriving is appropriately named 86251 *The Birmingham Post* with a terminating service from London Euston. This loco was withdrawn from service in the early 2000s but somehow managed to avoid scrapping until January 2023! 10 July 1991.

The revised version of Inter-City livery really seemed to suit these locos. This is 86258 *Talyllyn – The First Preserved Railway* arriving with another terminating service. At one point during the early 2000s, conversion to a battery/electric loco was on the cards but this never got off the ground and it was scrapped in December 2009. 10 July 1991.

Also suiting the class very well was the bright red Virgin Trains livery. This is 86260 *Driver Wallace Oakes GC* with another service from London Euston. This loco later received the number 86702 and Europhoenix livery plus the name *Cassiopeia* but, unfortunately, it never really got going on the UK network and was exported to Bulgaria in the mid-2010s. 23 June 2001.

Some of the similarities and differences between classes 86 and 87 can be appreciated here as 86248 *County of Clwyd / Sir Clwyd* and 87024 *Lord of the Isles* stand side-by-side at the station. The Class 86 was exported to Hungary in early 2009 and the Class 87 was scrapped in November 2005. 16 June 1993.

Here we see plain parcels red-liveried 86239 *L S Lowry* with 1M01, the 05.40 Poole to Liverpool Lime Street which it had worked from Coventry. Unfortunately, this loco was written off and scrapped, due to its involvement in a crash near Stafford in March 1996. 17 September 1991.

On to London Euston now as we see 86236 *Josiah Wedgwood–Master Potter 1736–1795* awaiting departure. This loco was always recognisable during this period, as it was the only member of the class to carry a light blue nameplate. It was scrapped in December 2003. 29 August 1996.

86231 *Starlight Express* has just been released after the departure of a northbound express and will probably run to Willesden Depot. This loco was exported to Bulgaria in the late 2000s. 29 August 1996.

The loco holding sidings were usually a good place to find 86s stabled between duties. This is Railfreight Distribution-liveried 86428 *Aldaniti* and parcels red 86430 just moving away. The fate of 86428 was detailed earlier, whilst 86430 was scrapped in December 2005. 26 May 1993.

Right: BR blue-liveried 86261 *Driver John Axon GC* is preparing to depart with a northbound express. Note the motor rail van behind. This loco was scrapped during November 2002. 9 August 1985.

Below: We now move down the line to Watford Junction, which was one of my go-to locations for the AC locos, not only 86s, and feature prominently in this book! This is 86101 *Sir William A Stanier FRS* just arrived with a northbound express from London Euston. This is one of the fortunate locos to survive into preservation and is currently main-line registered with Locomotive Services LTD (LSL). It can occasionally be seen hauling charter trains in the livery it is seen wearing here. 29 July 1994.

Arriving at the southern end of the station is 86204 *City of Carlisle* with another northbound service. This loco was scrapped during July 2003. 27 February 1990.

Three years later and 86204 *City of Carlisle* is now in the revised Inter-City 'Swallow' livery. It is seen here on the rear of a London Euston-bound service. Most of these expresses were hauled north by the loco, with the Driving Van Trailer (DVT) leading to London. 25 August 1993.

This is 86226 *Royal Mail Midlands* (formerly *Mail*) slowing for the station stop with a London Euston-bound service. Although withdrawn from service in 2002, this loco was not scrapped until April 2011. 22 July 1992.

With the prominent name board reminding us that this station was part of the Network Southeast regime at the time, this is 86209 *City of Coventry*, coming to a stand with a northbound service from London Euston. This loco was scrapped during July 2005. 27 February 1990.

Still very much a feature at this time was the running of parcels/mail trains. This very long example is approaching from the south, hauled by 86439. This loco (as 86639) has recently been exported to Bulgaria for further use by Freightliner. 27 February 1990.

In contrast to the previous shot, 86437 is heading south with a few flat wagons in tow. Note the permanent-way men to the left. Although at the time they were not doing anything wrong, I doubt very much that similar working conditions would be permitted in this day and age, without the appropriate contemporary safety regulations and red tape. This is another loco to have been exported to Bulgaria in 2023, in this case as 86637. 27 February 1990.

There is always an exception to the rule! As mentioned earlier, the DVT was usually leading to London, but 86212 *Preston Guild* is attached to 82127 as they pass the station on their way to Euston. I suspect some sort of fault on the DVT prevented it from being driven, necessitating that the loco run round from the rear. The loco was withdrawn in 2003 but lingered on until being scrapped in 2011, whilst the DVT is currently stored pending further use by LSL. 27 February 1990.

Unusually carrying no logos or branding, 86403 passes through with a northbound train. After renumbering to 86603, this loco was scrapped in December 2005. 27 February 1990.

On this particular Sunday, the main lines through the station were closed for planned works and all trains were using the 'slow' lines. This is Virgin Trains-liveried 86229 *Lions Club International* (formerly *Sir John Betjeman*), coming to a stop with a northbound train. This is another loco that lingered for ages in an increasingly dilapidated state from 2003 until finally being scrapped during 2020. 15 July 2001.

86233 *Laurence Olivier* looks smart in the earlier version of Inter-City livery as it speeds south with a Euston-bound express. 27 February 1990.

More than 12 years later, the same loco that featured in the previous shot looks rather different. 86233 *Alstom Heritage* is approaching with a northbound express from London Euston. In acknowledgement of the impending end of these locos on passenger service on the West Coast Main Line (WCML), it was repainted into the 'electric blue' livery carried when the locos were new. Perhaps surprisingly, this loco never made it into preservation, being withdrawn during 2003, and although exported to Bulgaria, it served only as spare parts until finally scrapped in 2019. 4 July 2002.

A couple of liners to end this Watford series of images, as we see 86620+86622 passing through with a northbound service. 86620 (later *Philip G Walton*) was scrapped during 2005, but 86622 was exported to Bulgaria for further use in 2023. 25 August 1993.

Heading south through the up local line with an unidentified freight is 86627 *The Industrial Society*. It is carrying the very short-lived Railfreight General livery, which was applied to very few locos (of any type) before being absorbed into the more familiar Railfreight Distribution style after about two years, and this loco may well have been one of the last to carry it. 86627 was exported to Bulgaria during 2023. 27 February 1990.

Over to the East of England now. This is BR blue 86249 *County of Merseyside*, just coupled up to a Norwich-bound express at London Liverpool Street. This loco was scrapped during October 2005. 17 January 1986.

Waiting on an adjacent platform is 86210 *City of Edinburgh* with the train preceding the one headed by 86249, which I caught to Ipswich. Details of the fate of this loco were noted earlier in this volume. 17 January 1986.

At this point in time, electrification of the Great Eastern Main Line (GEML) had only reached Ipswich, from where diesel traction then took over for the continuation to Norwich. 86210 *City of Edinburgh* is seen again, this time running through the middle road after being detached from my train from Liverpool Street. 17 January 1986.

Almost exactly 15 years later, this is 86238 *European Community*, now wearing the turquoise Anglia livery and waiting to depart Ipswich with a Norwich to London Liverpool Street service. 27 January 2001.

Just peeking out from the shadow of the station buildings is 86217 *City University* (formerly *Halley's Comet* and, before that, *Comet*) with another service bound for London Liverpool Street. This loco was exported to Hungary in 2013 and is currently in frontline service. 27 January 2001.

At the same spot but with no such shadow issues, this is 86246 (formerly *Royal Anglian Regiment),* also awaiting departure for London Liverpool Street. Upon withdrawal in 2004, this loco was used as a source of spares for AC locos that were preserved, or being preserved, at the time, and was not finally scrapped until 2017. 27 January 2001.

Class 86s were also staple motive power for the various electric-hauled liner services in the area and were regularly to be seen stabled by the station at Ipswich. Due to it being a Saturday when I visited, there were perhaps more on view than a normal weekday, which is borne out by this sight of 86633 *Wulfruna* + 86621 *London School of Economics* + 86612 *Elizabeth Garrett Anderson* + 866xx + 86627 + 86628 *Aldaniti* + 866xx, all awaiting their next duties. Of these locos, 86633/86621 were both scrapped in 2013, and 86612/86627/86628 were exported to Bulgaria during 2023. 27 January 2001.

A few freight services now to conclude this GEML series. This is 86607+86639 crossing the low viaduct over the river Stour at Cattawade, near Manningtree, with a northbound liner from Felixstowe. Both of these locos were exported to Bulgaria during 2023. 29 May 2014.

The use of a powerful telephoto lens here at Colchester emphasises the considerable undulating gradient on the approach to the station, as 86501 is viewed passing with a northbound service. For some years, this was a unique machine modified by re-gearing and was often seen working solo. It was exported to Bulgaria (after being converted back to 86608) in 2023. 20 October 2011.

Not long before being stood down in late 2020, 86637+86622 pass Stratford with 4M87, the 11.13 Felixstowe to Trafford Park. Both of these locos were exported to Bulgaria during 2023. 29 April 2019.

Moving back to the WCML, we see 86228 *Vulcan Heritage* in the revised Inter-City livery, waiting to depart from Stafford with a London Euston-bound service. This loco was withdrawn from service in 2003 but was exported to Hungary in 2013 and is still in service. 22 April 1992.

Hardwicke

86225 *Hardwicke* in revised Inter-City livery arrives at Stockport with a Manchester Piccadilly to London Euston service. This loco was scrapped during 2006. 7 April 1993.

Virgin-liveried 86247 *Abraham Darby* is seen coming into Coventry with a London Euston to Birmingham New Street service. This loco was withdrawn during 2003 but two cabs have been preserved by private individuals, with the rest of the loco being scrapped during 2015. 20 February 2003.

Leaning into the curve at Oxenholme in the Lake District is Virgin-liveried 86242 *James Kennedy GC*, with a London Euston to Glasgow Central train. This loco was exported to Hungary during 2013 and remains in service for Floyd Zrt.
17 September 2000.

Plain parcels red 86239 *L S Lowry* has just arrived at Edinburgh with a terminating cross-country service. This loco was unfortunately written off in a serious accident that occurred near Stafford in early 1996.
27 August 1992.

Just boarding at Glasgow Central is 1O16, the 12.30 to Poole, with Virgin red-liveried 86244 *The Royal British Legion* up front. The loco worked this train to Birmingham New Street, from where a Class 47 took over for the remainder of the journey. The loco was scrapped during 2003.
29 September 2000.

A series of freight services now, starting with this image of Freightliner green-liveried pair 86621+86639 passing the delightfully named location of Cow Roast on the WCML, just south of Tring, with a service bound for Felixstowe. Just a month after this image was taken, 86621 was withdrawn in April 2011 and was scrapped in 2013, whilst 86639 was exported to Bulgaria in 2023. 4 March 2011.

Heading in the opposite direction is a northbound liner headed by 86609+86637. The leading loco is in the first version of Freightliner green, whilst the train loco is in what was then the latest 'Powerhaul' livery. Both of these locos were exported to Bulgaria in 2023. 4 March 2011.

Almost right behind the train seen in the previous shot, solo 86501 also heads north with an unidentified liner. Due to the often solo working of this loco, it gained the nickname 'Billy No Mates'! 4 March 2011.

86501 is seen again, this time heading south through Rugeley Trent Valley station with a well-loaded liner. This is a popular station for photographers, due to the long sweeping curve and the reverse curves to the south of the station. 22 October 2009.

Another southbound liner is captured heading through the up main line at Bletchley, with 86622+86615 *Rotary International* at the sharp end. 86622 is still in the Freightliner grey livery, whilst 86615 is in standard green. The locos have had very different futures, with 622 being exported to Bulgaria in 2023, whilst 615 was scrapped during 2007. 20 February 2003.

Also at Bletchley on the same day are 86631+86602, both in original Freightliner green livery and heading south on the up relief line. Six months after the date of this shot, 86631 was written off in a crash at Norton Bridge, south of Crewe, in October 2003, whilst 86602 fared only slightly better, being withdrawn in 2005 and scrapped in 2010. 20 February 2003.

We are at Stafford now to see 86612+86639 passing through with a northbound service from Felixstowe. Both of these locos were exported to Bulgaria in 2023. 4 February 2016.

Headstone Lane station, located on the outskirts of north London, is reached by regular London Overground services. Just to the north of the station is a convenient footbridge from which I took this shot of 86632+86627 (formerly *The Industrial Society*) heading south with an unidentified liner. These are another two locos exported to Bulgaria in 2023. 27 May 2011.

Not far from Headstone Lane is Harrow & Wealdstone, the scene of the terrible crash of 1952, where we see 86638+86604 powering north with a liner from Felixstowe. This was yet another pair of locos to be exported to Bulgaria in 2023. 5 November 2010.

Our last view of an 86-hauled liner is at Tring, where we see a 'worm's-eye view' of 86602+86622 heading for Felixstowe. The fate of both these locos was detailed earlier. 10 July 2003.

During the 2000s, when many of the class were being withdrawn from frontline passenger service, Network Rail acquired three locos to act as mobile load banks to test the overhead wires. I believe they also found use as 'icebreakers' during the winter months as a means of ensuring that the wires were kept free of ice and snow. One or two locos could often be found stabled at York during the day. This is bright yellow 86902 *Rail Vehicle Engineering* in one of the bay platforms at the south end of the station. Unfortunately, the loco was scrapped during 2016, but one cab has survived, being purchased by a private individual. 20 February 2008.

RAIL VEHICLE
ENGINEERING

To conclude this section on Class 86s is 86401 (the former 86001) in three different liveries. First, we see the loco in immaculate Network SouthEast livery, in Basingstoke down yard of all places during the popular Railfair of 1987. This was the only member of the class to carry this livery in service. It was withdrawn in 2002, secured for preservation in 2004, and at the time of writing, finds itself in occasional main line service with West Coast Railways (WCRC), carrying the dark blue Caledonian Sleeper livery from its time acting as shunt loco at London Euston in the late 2010s. 26 September 1987.

Second, we see what must be a contender for the shortest parcels train, with the loco looking quite smart in Rail Express Systems (RES) livery as it hauls just one vehicle southbound through Watford Junction. 25 August 1993.

And finally, we see the loco at Watford Junction again, this time on the rear of a London Euston-bound express. It is in English, Welsh & Scottish (EWS) livery, which I believe only two Class 86 locos carried, and carrying the name *Hertfordshire Railtours*.

Chapter 2

Class 87

To start our look at Class 87s, we are at Crewe again for a series of images starting with the first loco of the class, 87001 *Royal Scot*, passing through with a London Euston to Glasgow express. Upon withdrawal, this loco was donated to the National Railway Museum in York, where it can be seen on static display in its original BR blue livery. 7 April 1993.

Soon after the station track remodelling, 87011 *The Black Prince* is pulling away with a northbound express. This loco was scrapped during 2010. 9 August 1985.

This time we see 87003 *Patriot* waiting to depart for London Euston. This is one of a few locos that was exported to Bulgaria in the late 2000s and is still in service there. 9 August 1985.

Arriving with a service from London Euston, 87016 *Willesden Inter-City Depot* (formerly *Sir Francis Drake*) is seen gliding to a halt with a Glasgow-bound train formed of a smart rake of Mk 3 coaches. This loco has the dubious record of being the first Class 87/0 to be scrapped (though not the first withdrawn from service) during 2004. 7 April 1993.

Above: Approaching from the north is 87023 with 1A40, the 09.28 Carlisle to London Euston. The loco (formerly *Highland Chieftain*) is seen during a three-year period without a name. Not long after this shot was taken, however, it received the name *Velocity*. The loco has since been exported to Bulgaria. 9 August 1985.

Right: Another rake of Mk 3s heading north arrives behind 87030 *Black Douglas*. This loco was scrapped during 2010. 7 April 1993.

Having just undergone a crew change, 87035 *Robert Burns* is preparing to head north with a train from London Euston. This was the first loco to find its way into preservation when it was handed over to the Crewe Heritage Centre during September 2005. 9 August 1985.

Eleven years later and 87035 *Robert Burns* had received the revised Inter-City livery. It is waiting to depart with a train for Liverpool. 5 June 1996.

Quite an unusual sight this time as 87034 *William Shakespeare* is seen approaching the station off the unelectrified line from Chester with what is believed to be a diverted 1O21, the 09.05 Glasgow Central to Poole service, which had been dragged between Warrington Bank Quay and Crewe by 25268 of all things! The reason for the diversion is not known, but possibly relates to the overhead catenary. 9 August 1985.

Two northbound services are seen here waiting to depart. 87018 *Lord Nelson* is on the left with a train for Glasgow and 87013 *John O' Gaunt* is on the right with a Liverpool train. 87018 was scrapped during 2010, but 87013 was exported to Bulgaria in 2009. 7 April 1993.

This time, 87032 *Kenilworth* is powering through the down through line with a London Euston to Glasgow Central non-stop express. Unfortunately, this loco was reduced to a pile of scrap during 2010. 9 August 1985.

Looking a bit tatty in its original version of Inter-City livery, this is 87026 *Sir Richard Arkwright* (formerly *Redgauntlet*) awaiting departure. This loco was exported to Bulgaria in 2009. 7 April 1993.

Some ten years later, 87018 *Lord Nelson* + 90010 *275 Railway Squadron (Volunteers)* are departing on the rear of a service bound for London Euston. The reason for this pair was probably due to the failure of the Class 90. The Class 87 was in its final year of service, but the Class 90 is still in service on the UK network today, now operated by Freightliner. 31 May 2003.

This is the unique 87101 *Stephenson* passing through the station light engine. Although outwardly, the loco appeared the same as the rest of the Class 87 fleet, there were major internal differences, particularly where the electrical control equipment was concerned. It worked for a number of years alongside the main fleet but was transferred to the Railfreight sector in the late 1980s and restricted to 75mph. After being taken over by EWS, it was rarely used and was eventually withdrawn during 1999. Perhaps surprisingly, it was scrapped during 2002. However, some of the unique internal components were saved, I believe. 5 June 1996.

Mentioned earlier, the nearby Crewe Works has held many a popular open day over the years, and here is immaculate 87001 on display in the almost original as-built condition in which it was repainted for its last months in frontline service. 31 May 2003.

This is a bit different! 87002 is seen at the same open day as the previous shot, resplendent in Porterbrook purple/white livery that it carried for a while in service. This loco has since been preserved by Locomotive Services LTD (LSL), returned to Inter-City 'Swallow' livery and reunited with its *Royal Sovereign* nameplates. It can now sometimes be seen working charter trains on the main line. 31 May 2003.

City of Liverpool

Moving further south on the WCML, we come to Rugby station, where we see a snapshot of the procession of electric locos working northbound in a short space of time on this summer day in 2004. This one is Virgin-liveried 87008 *City of Liverpool*, passing through with a fine matching rake of Mk3 stock and a driving van trailer (DVT) on the rear. This loco was exported to Bulgaria in 2008, but I believe it is currently out of service and being used for spares. 23 July 2004.

Next up is 87010 *King Arthur* at the same location and with another rake of Mk3s heading north on the through line. The station here used to have an overall roof across the tracks, and a couple of the chopped-off stumps of the original steel pillars can be seen just by the engine. This loco was also exported to Bulgaria during 2008. 23 July 2004.

Seen earlier at the Crewe Works open day, purple-liveried 87002 is the next one to be captured heading north. The details of this loco were set out earlier. 23 July 2004.

Another Virgin-liveried example, 87021 *Robert the Bruce* has a train of more matching Mk3s making for the north. This loco was scrapped during 2010. 23 July 2004.

Our last shot from Rugby sees 87028 (formerly *Lord President*) pulling into the station with a northbound stopping service. This image was taken during a three-year period that the loco spent nameless, although it was to regain this name in 2006. It was exported to Bulgaria in 2009. 23 July 2004.

Moving further south again to Watford Junction for another short series, we first see 87019 *Winston Churchill* + 82141 approaching from the north with a service for London Euston. There was obviously some sort of problem with the DVT for the loco to be leading towards the capital. This loco was exported to Bulgaria during 2009. 4 July 2002.

This is 87004 *Britannia* heading along the down local line through the station with a northbound express. This is another loco that was exported to Bulgaria in 2009 and I believe it still carries its original name and even sports BR blue livery. 15 July 2001.

Wearing a rather battered original Inter-City livery, 87017 *Iron Duke* is drawing to a halt with a northbound service. This loco was exported to Bulgaria during 2009, and is another one retaining its original name. 25 August 1993.

Conversely, a very smart-looking 87021 *Robert the Bruce* in revised Inter-City livery is seen calling with a northbound service. Details for the fate of this loco were set out earlier. 25 August 1993.

87035 *Robert Burns* is seen about to propel a London Euston-bound express away from the station. This loco can now be seen in immaculate Virgin Trains red livery, on static display at the Crewe Heritage Centre. 25 August 1993.

Another service for London Euston departs south, propelled by Virgin-liveried 87013 *John O'Gaunt*. This is the only Class 87 ever to have visited Bournemouth, when it was an exhibit at the open day held at Bournemouth West Depot in September 1992. This is another loco that was exported to Bulgaria during 2009. 4 July 2002.

Southbound main line services often only called at the station to drop off passengers, with the local stopping services providing the means to board here. This is 87027 *Wolf of Badenoch* in revised Inter-City livery on the rear of another London Euston-bound service. This name was transferred to 90002 in the early 2020s. After being used as a source of spares for those locos then being exported to Bulgaria, it was scrapped during 2010. 3 April 1997.

This is Virgin-liveried 87032 *Kenilworth* speeding north with a service from London Euston. The fate of this loco was noted earlier. 4 July 2002.

Northbound main line services booked to stop here were just to pick up passengers and not to drop off, the opposite of southbound trains. Ten years before the previous image, we see 87012 *The Royal Bank of Scotland* at the same spot calling for custom. This loco was originally named *Coeur de Lion* back in 1978, and it regained these plates after the ones seen here were removed in the early 2000s. However, in the mid-2000s it was repainted in Network SouthEast (NSE) livery and again renamed *The Olympian* for around a year or so until it was exported to Bulgaria in 2009, still carrying NSE livery but not the name. 22 July 1992.

Winding up our visit to Watford Junction, we see 87003 *Patriot* + 87020 *North Briton* racing south with a Freightliner service. At this time, the two locos would have been replaced by a diesel loco at Wembley Yard. The use of a pair of 87s on a freight train was not that common back then. Note that the first loco is in revised Inter-City livery, whilst the train loco is still in the original version. The fate of 87003 was detailed earlier, whilst 87020 was exported to Bulgaria in 2009. 27 February 1990.

Moving much further north, this is the first of a few images from Carlisle. Returned to BR blue livery for its last months in service, this is pioneer 87001 *Royal Scot* approaching with a service from London Euston to Glasgow Central. The name applied to this loco was originally *Stephenson* back in 1978 but it has swapped back and forth a couple of times with *Royal Scot*. I think it is now both! Details for this loco appeared earlier in this book. 29 December 2003.

87007 *City of Manchester* is seen receding into the distance as it propels a Glasgow Central to London Euston service away from the station. The lines diverging to the left lead to Newcastle and also to the famous Settle and Carlisle line (S&C). This loco was exported to Bulgaria during 2008. 30 January 2004.

Occasionally main line services were double-headed or in this case, double-pushed! I suspect the train loco here had been declared a failure at some point. 87006 *George Reynolds* + 87021 *Robert the Bruce* are heading away to London Euston. 87021 was detailed earlier, but 87006 (formerly *City of Glasgow* and *Glasgow Garden Festival*) was one of the last examples withdrawn during December 2006 and was exported to Bulgaria in 2009. 29 December 2003.

Curving towards the station this time is 87024 *Lord of the Isles* with a London Euston to Glasgow Central express. Unfortunately, this was one of the first of the class to be scrapped during 2005. 2 February 2004.

Heading back south, we are at Birmingham New Street to see BR blue 87031 *Hal o' The Wynd* pulling away with a train for London Euston. Note the newspapers acting as a sun visor, a common practice by drivers in this era! Unfortunately, this loco was reduced to scrap during 2010. *Circa* 1988.

This station has always been pretty tricky for photography, being as it is mostly beneath a huge shopping centre! This is 87014 *Knight of the Thistle* arriving with a terminating service from London Euston. This loco was exported to Bulgaria during 2009.

Peering out from the gloom is 87017 *Iron Duke*, just arrived with a cross country service. The loco would either have come off the train here or worked as far as Coventry, depending on the destination. Details for this loco were given earlier in this book. 29 August 1996.

Howard of Effingham

Finding a little bit of daylight, this is 87015 *Howard of Effingham*, just arrived with a train from London Euston. This was another early casualty, being scrapped during 2005. 19 November 1998.

Leaving the gloom of New Street, this is 87030 *Black Douglas* speeding north through Tring with a train from London Euston. At the time, no main-line services were booked to call here. Details for this loco were noted earlier in the book. 19 July 2003.

Black Douglas

Although no main-line services stopped here, this one did briefly for a signal check and I managed to grab this shot before 87014 *Knight of the Thistle* continued propelling its train onwards to London Euston. 19 July 2003.

A very battered-looking 87005 *City of London* hauls another northbound service from London Euston. Just two months after this image was taken, the loco became the first of the class to be withdrawn from service. It was scrapped during 2005. 19 July 2003.

At this time 87022 *Cock O' The North* was the last of the class to wear the original BR blue livery. It is seen here waiting for the right away at Wolverhampton with a London Euston-bound service. This loco was exported to Bulgaria in 2009. 28 September 1988.

The original Inter-City livery is looking weather-worn as 87024 *Lord of the Isles* is seen arriving at Wolverhampton in the opposite direction with a northbound cross-country service. 28 September 1988.

Racing south through Stafford is 87029 *Earl Marischal* with a train from Glasgow Central to London Euston. It is interesting to note that the signal the train has just passed has already returned to a red aspect. This loco was exported to Bulgaria during 2009. 22 April 1992.

On the same day, 87017 *Iron Duke* is drawing to a halt with a northbound express. In the present day, there are a regular amount of main-line services that call here. 22 April 1992.

Complete with gold-painted buffers applied at Wembley Depot, a smart-looking 87006 (formerly *George Reynolds*) is seen here arriving at Coventry in failing light with 1G21, the 16.52 London Euston to Birmingham New Street service. This train was one of the final Virgin loco-hauled services to remain on the WCML. 21 September 2006.

Still at Coventry, but a couple of years earlier, we see 87019 *Sir Winston Churchill*, with a liberal number of splatted flies on the cab end, arriving with a service from London Euston to Birmingham New Street. 23 July 2004.

Here we see 87026 *Sir Richard Arkwright* (formerly *Redgauntlet*) arriving at Bletchley with a northbound express. 20 February 2003.

Also approaching Bletchley on the same day is 87027 *Wolf of Badenoch* with a service from London Euston to Glasgow Central. On this day, a points problem developed just to the south of the station and a few main-line services were diverted through the station via the down local line. 20 February 2003.

This time we see 87024 *Lord of the Isles* again, arriving at Stockport with a London Euston to Manchester Piccadilly service. Note the long-vanished electric unit in the distance. 7 April 1993.

On the 'stops' at Glasgow Central is 87035 *Robert Burns*, which is waiting to propel a service south to London Euston. 29 September 2000.

Above: At the other end of the WCML, we are now at London Euston, where we see 87020 *North Briton* awaiting departure with a northbound express. 22 July 1992.

Left: For many years, this was a regular sight at London Euston as 87026 *Sir Richard Arkwright* (formerly *Redgauntlet*) and 87013 *John O'Gaunt* wait side by side for departure with expresses for the north of England. Which one would you have gone for? 26 May 1993.

On the same day as the previous shot, this is a study of 87031 *Hal o' the Wynd* awaiting its next duty at London Euston. 26 May 1993.

Upon withdrawal during 2005, 87001 *Royal Scot* was claimed by the National Railway Museum and is now a static exhibit. The immaculate loco is seen here in its earlier days of preservation inside the main museum building. 21 February 2008.

Something very unusual to end this section on Class 87s. The Hampshire town of Basingstoke is not a location you would immediately associate with overhead electric locos, but this is 47810 *Crewe Diesel Depot*, hauling 86101 *Sir William A Stanier FRS* + 87002 *Royal Sovereign* through the station as 0Z20, the 08.23 Crewe H.S. to Eastleigh Arlington. Both of these locos were used by Caledonian Sleeper services for a while and this unusual move was carried out after that had ended. The locos were heading to the paint shop at Eastleigh for transforming into Inter-City livery. Although this location was undoubtedly a first for an 87, amazingly this is not the first time a Class 86 has been here, as 86401 was displayed at the Basingstoke Railfair at the end of September 1987! See the Class 86 section. 19 November 2019.

Chapter 3

Class 90

The first of the class, 90001 *BBC Midlands Today*, is awaiting departure north from Crewe. Now preserved in main line running condition with LSL under the name *Royal Scot*, this loco has regained the original Inter-City livery in which it is seen here, but rarely sees use at the present time. 5 June 1996.

Staying at Crewe for a while, this is 90013 *The Law Society* passing through the down fast line with a London Euston to Glasgow Central express. After going on to work with Virgin Trains and Anglia, this loco is now in service with Freightliner in that company's latest orange and black livery. 7 April 1993.

90017 (later *Rail Express Systems – Quality Assured*) was one of the locos that moved from working Inter-City trains to the parcels sector in the late 1990s. It is seen here in the appropriate red RES livery, waiting to depart south with an unidentified service. This loco was put into open storage as long ago as 2006, and it is doubtful that it will ever see service again. 7 April 1993.

This is 90015 *BBC North West*, about to leave with a northbound train from London Euston. This was another loco that worked for Virgin and Anglia before being taken on by Freightliner, with which it is still in service today, though not carrying a name. 7 April 1993.

Next we see 90002 *The Girls Brigade* awaiting to depart with a northbound train. This is another loco that went on to work with Virgin and Anglia, but upon withdrawal from the latter services, it entered preservation with LSL and is kept immaculate in the livery seen here, bearing the name *Wolf of Badenoch* originally carried by 87027. To date, it has been used a little more than 90001 on various charter services. 5 June 1996.

In full Virgin Trains livery, 90012 *British Transport Police* is arriving with a train from London Euston. This loco later went on to work for Anglia and is currently in service with Freightliner. 31 May 2003.

Moving to the East of England, we start a section showing the class on various workings in that part of the UK. In the colourful 'one' (formerly Anglia) livery, 90014 *Norfolk and Norwich Festival* awaits departure from Norwich with a train for London Liverpool Street. This loco is still in service today, working for Freightliner and named *Over the Rainbow*. 16 March 2007.

On the same day, sister loco 90015 has just arrived at Norwich from London Liverpool Street and is disgorging passengers. This loco is now in service with Freightliner. 16 March 2007.

During their time working the Great Eastern Main Line (GEML) services, the locos underwent a few operator changes that were sometimes tricky to keep up with! Here is 90004 with the 'one' insignia removed, also awaiting departure from Norwich for London Liverpool Street in the period just after National Express took over. This is another loco now at work with Freightliner. 20 June 2008.

A few years later and National Express turned into Greater Anglia. That transition is evident here at Norwich with 90005 *Vice Admiral Lord Nelson* to the left in the new Greater Anglia livery, whilst 90002 *Eastern Daily Press 1870–2010 Serving Norfolk for 140 Years* to the right is still in Anglia/National Express colours but with Greater Anglia branding. 90005 is now working for Freightliner, and 90002 for LSL. 22 February 2014.

It was perhaps inevitable that some of the locos used on the GEML services would from time to time suffer failures, so other locos were occasionally hired in to cover. This is 90036 in a hybrid Railfreight/EWS livery, stabled at Norwich in case of problems with the main fleet. This loco was in service with DBC until February 2023, when it was put into storage at Crewe Electric Depot. 20 June 2008.

This is 90007 *Sir John Betjeman*, just drawing to a halt at Ipswich with a Norwich to London Liverpool Street service. This loco carried on in service until loco-hauled services ended on the GEML in early 2020, after which they were replaced by Class 745 units. 29 May 2014.

90012 *Royal Anglian Regiment* is approaching Ipswich with another Norwich to London Liverpool Street service. Freightliner's 90044 is seen to the right, stabled awaiting its next duty. 90012 is also now working for Freightliner. 29 May 2014.

Receding into the distance at Ipswich is 90013 (formerly *The Law Society*) with another London Liverpool to Norwich train. This loco also now works for Freightliner. 29 May 2014.

In the rather dull-looking original Freightliner livery, 90048 is seen on the stabling point at Ipswich. This loco looks much brighter today in the latest orange and black Freightliner livery. 29 May 2014.

Complete with a large Union flag on the bodyside, this is 90009 *Diamond Jubilee* coming across the river Stour bridge at Cattawade on the approach to Manningtree, with a Norwich to London Liverpool Street express. This loco is now working for Freightliner and can still regularly be seen at this location, but now hauling containers rather than people. 29 May 2014.

Another Norwich to London Liverpool Street service comes across the Cattawade Viaduct with 90011 *East Anglian Daily Times Suffolk and Proud* up front. This is another loco now operating with Freightliner. 29 May 2014.

Staying on the GEML, this is the first of a few images taken at Colchester station. 90001 (formerly *BBC Midlands Today*) is first up as it propels a Norwich-bound service away on the next leg of its journey. 20 October 2011.

At the London end of the station is 90012 *Royal Anglian Regiment*, waiting to depart with another express bound for London Liverpool Street. 20 October 2011.

90007 *Sir John Betjeman* brakes for the station stop on the rear of a Norwich-bound service. Colchester holds the record for the longest station platform in the UK, although the platform is actually split in two these days. 20 October 2011.

Back at the eastern end of the station again, we see 90008 *The East Anglian* in National Express livery approaching with an express for London Liverpool Street. This is yet another loco that is now working for Freightliner. 20 October 2011.

Either failed or on standby duties is 90010 *Bressingham Steam & Gardens,* unusually stabled in the up engineers siding at the station. Yes, you have guessed it, another loco now working with Freightliner. 20 October 2011.

The view to the east of the station is quite superb, especially when using a zoom lens. 90003 *Raedwald of East Anglia* is approaching the station stop with a London Liverpool Street express, just as 70001 *Powerhaul* departs with a Felixstowe-bound liner. 90003 itself now works for Freightliner. 20 October 2011.

Running eastbound light engine, this is EWS-liveried 90026 (formerly *Crewe International Electric Maintenance Depot*) which is probably on hire to National Express to cover any problems with its fleet, much as with 90036 earlier. This particular loco was put into store by DBC in February 2023. 20 October 2011.

The effect of the gradient change is clearly seen here as 90016 approaches with a well-loaded Freightliner service from Felixstowe, bound for Crewe. This is one of a handful of the class that have never carried names. It remains in service with Freightliner today but is now in orange and black livery. 20 October 2011.

A broadside view of 90049 in the down reception loop displaying the latest (at the time) Freightliner 'Powerhaul' livery. A number of examples were painted in this scheme until it was superseded by the now standard orange and black. At the time of writing, only a few of the class still retain this livery. 20 October 2011.

Another Freightliner service, but this time hauled through the down main line by two-tone grey-liveried 90047. This loco has since been repainted in the latest orange and black Freightliner livery. 20 October 2011.

Beneath a tangle of overhead wires, we see 90003 *Raedwald of East Anglia* and 90004 *Eastern Daily Press 1870–2010 Serving Norfolk for 140 Years* (a name later carried by 90002) captured with up and down expresses to/from Norwich and London, alongside 321319 on a local service from Colchester Town, just east of the station. 20 October 2011.

For the last few views on the GEML we are at Stratford, east London, during the final full year of loco haulage. This is a now un-named 90013 in the final white and grey livery worn by the class when operating for Greater Anglia, propelling a London Liverpool Street to Norwich service. This loco is now in Freightliner orange and black livery. 29 April 2019.

90011 *East Anglian Daily Times Suffolk & Proud* passes through with a London Liverpool to Norwich service. This is another loco that is now operating for Freightliner in orange and black livery. 29 April 2019.

Another un-named example at the time was 90009 (formerly *The Economist* and *Royal Show*), seen passing through the station with a Liverpool Street service. Once again, this loco now works for Freightliner and carries that firm's latest orange and black livery. 29 April 2019.

This time we see 90014 *Norfolk and Norwich Festival* passing through on the rear of a London-bound service. This loco is now in orange and black Freightliner livery and named *Over the Rainbow*. 29 April 2019.

The final GEML shot sees 90002 *Eastern Daily Press 1870–2010 – Serving Norfolk for 140 Years* passing on the rear of another express bound for Norwich. The loco is now back in Inter-City livery with LSL and named *Wolf of Badenoch*. 29 April 2019.

We now head back to the WCML and Watford Junction, where we see 90004 *D'Oyly Carte Opera Company* in its original Inter-City livery, passing through with a London Euston to Glasgow Central service. The loco was only around five years old at this point and one of the mainstays of WCML services. 22 July 1992.

With almost ten years of service under its belt, 90004 is now in Virgin Trains red livery and named *City of Glasgow* as it stands in the same spot as the previous shot, again with a northbound service. 4 July 2002.

90001 *BBC Midlands Today* is captured heading north from the station on the up local line with a train from London Euston. The main lines in the foreground were temporarily closed for planned maintenance on this day. 15 July 2001.

Looking south from the station, a two-year-old 90006 (later *High Sheriff*) approaches with an express from London Euston. As mentioned earlier in this book, only a few Inter-City services stopped here, northbound to pick up and southbound to drop off. 27 February 1990.

Though it doesn't look like it is even newer at less than a year of age, 90019 (later *Penny Black*) is calling with a northbound train. This loco was withdrawn from service during July 2023 by DBC, the reason given at the time apparently being that these locos are too costly to run. 27 February 1990.

Eleven-month-old 90026 (later *Crewe Electric Depot*, then *Crewe International Electric Maintenance Depot*) carrying mainline livery is also arriving from the south, hauling a combination of Mk1 and Mk2 stock. By this time, Mk1 stock on Inter-City services was quite unusual. This was another loco withdrawn from service by DBC during July 2023. 27 February 1990.

Next built loco 90027 (later *Allerton T&RS Depot*) is wearing the same livery as it departs south on the rear of a London Euston-bound express. This loco was withdrawn from service back in 2007 and is highly unlikely to work again. 27 February 1990.

Some of the class (90026-050) were modified during the 1990s, mainly to operate freight trains. These examples were reclassified as Class 90/1 (90126–150), but by the early 2000s many had reverted to their original numbers. A few months before reverting, 90142 is seen departing on the rear of an express for London Euston. This loco is currently in service (as 90042) with Freightliner, wearing the now obsolete 'Powerhaul' livery. 15 July 2001.

Leaving Watford Junction now, we are in the capital for this view of 90005 *Financial Times* + 86204 *City of Carlisle* + 87007 *City of Manchester*, combining the three main forms of Inter-City motive power at that time operating on the WCML. The '90' is now with Freightliner, the '86' was scrapped during 2003 and the '87' is currently at work in Bulgaria. 26 May 1993.

This is Tring station, where Rail Express Systems (RES)-liveried 90016 is captured speeding through with a northbound service. The RES livery was a pretty good match-up with the Virgin red livery and didn't look too out of place. This loco is still in use but now with Freightliner, currently wearing the latest orange and black livery. 20 July 2003.

In the early 2000s, it was not unusual to see RES/Freight Sector locos deputising for the normal Virgin examples on WCML expresses due to unavailability. This is Railfreight Distribution-liveried 90023, propelling a London Euston-bound express through the station at Tring again. This loco was stored as long ago as 2005, and the chances of it ever working again are very slim. 20 February 2003.

Although it doesn't look like it is almost new, here we see 90003 (later *The Herald*) soon after arrival at Wolverhampton with a service from London Euston. Note that the BREL works plate was still in situ at this time, below the running number. The loco is now with Freightliner and carries that firm's current orange and black livery. 28 September 1988.

Loco and stock are again in matching Virgin Trains livery as 90013 *The Law Society* is seen passing through Rugby with a London Euston to Glasgow Central service. This is another loco now at work with Freightliner. 23 July 2004.

During the late 2000s/early 2010s, Virgin Trains was using a set of Mk3 coaches often known as 'Pretendalino' for various timetabled and relief services on the WCML. This is 90036, rapidly approaching Harrow & Wealdstone with an unidentified northbound service from London Euston. This loco was withdrawn by DBC in 2023. 5 November 2010.

The 'Pretendalino' set is seen again, this time heading south past South Kenton behind 90048 in the old two-tone grey Freightliner livery. Today, this loco is still hard at work with Freightliner and is now in the latest orange and black livery. 27 May 2011.

Lastly, we see the set heading south at Cow Roast, just south of Tring, this time propelled by Freightliner 'Powerhaul'-liveried 90041. This loco is still in service with Freightliner, but now carries orange and black livery. 4 March 2011.

As recently as 2018, this is DBC-liveried 90019 *Multimodal*, approaching Alexandra Palace with 1B84, the 12.06 London King's Cross to Newark North Gate service. The loco was on hire to Virgin Trains East Coast at the time. 13 November 2018.

As mentioned earlier, during the 1990s some locos were reclassified as 90/1s, which involved isolating the Electric Train Supply (ETS), limiting the top speed from 110mph to 75mph and dedicating them to freight trains. Still carrying 'mainline' livery, this is 90136 (formerly 90036) passing Watford Junction with a southbound Freightliner service. 22 July 1992.

Passing slowly through Coventry is 90049, still in two-tone grey Freightliner livery, heading south with a liner. 20 September 2007.

90049 is now in almost ex-works 'Powerhaul' livery (now obsolete), heading north past Headstone Lane on the WCML with a fully loaded service. These days, it is unusual to see just one loco on these Freightliner trains. This particular loco is still working for Freightliner and, for the time being, remains in the livery seen here. 27 May 2011.

Virgin-liveried 90013 *The Law Society* is seen again, this time awaiting departure from Milton Keynes Central with a northbound service from London Euston. 20 February 2003.

Another loco hired in by Virgin Trains, English, Welsh & Scottish (EWS)-liveried 90034 approaches the down local platform at Bletchley with a northbound service. This loco was withdrawn by DBC in 2023. 20 February 2003.

Much further north at Carlisle, we see 90009 *The Economist* powering south from the station with a Glasgow Central to London Euston train. This loco now wears the latest orange and black livery operating for Freightliner, but is now un-named. 31 December 2003.

There is still a touch of frost on the sleepers as 90005 *Financial Times* is captured propelling another service away from Carlisle station towards London Euston. This is another example since to have been repainted in the latest orange and black livery of Freightliner. 31 December 2003.

Various locos could often be found stabled next to the station at Carlisle (and occasionally still can). This is 90039 in a very worn Railfreight Distribution livery awaiting its next working. After a few more livery changes and periods in storage, this loco received a one-off black livery with the slogan 'I am the Backbone of the Economy' and was named *The Chartered Institute of Logistics & Transport*. Unfortunately, it was withdrawn by DBC in mid-2023, supposedly being too costly to run! 31 December 2003.

In the same spot on the following day is EWS-liveried 90032 (formerly *Cerestar*). This was one of the earliest examples put into storage, just a month or so after this shot was taken. I doubt it will ever work again. 1 January 2004.

Further south again now, at the popular location of Stafford station. Approaching from the north is solo 90046 in original green Freightliner livery, heading south with an unidentified service. The loco still soldiers on in this livery at the time of writing, being the last of the class in these colours. 23 January 2009.

I have mentioned the latest Freightliner orange and black livery a few times so far and this is 90003 actually displaying this smart livery at Stafford, having just arrived on a light engine driver training run. 14 October 2022.

Commencing a short series depicting double-headed trains, we are still at Stafford, where we see 90047+90016 heading north with a service from Felixstowe. Both of these locos have since received orange and black livery. 13 February 2019.

Heading through Stafford in the opposite direction is 'Powerhaul' pair 90049+90045, with a Felixstowe-bound service. Both of these locos still wear this livery, but perhaps not for too much longer. 13 February 2019.

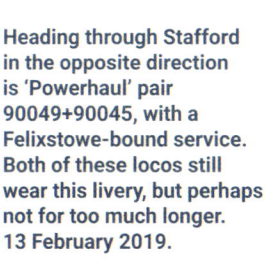

90046+90044 come to a stand at Ipswich with 4L89, the 04.10 Basford Hall to Felixstowe, to pick up the shunter before proceeding to the reception lines for a loco change. The two different Freightliner liveries make a striking comparison. 27 September 2023.

Having just departed the reception sidings at Ipswich, 90007+90012 are coming north through the station with 4M87, the 11.13 Felixstowe to Trafford Park service. 27 September 2023.

Heading south at Watford Junction are 90013+90049 with a slightly late running 4L89, the 04.10 Basford Hall to Felixstowe service. 28 September 2023.

In the opposite direction, 90011+90015 power north through Watford Junction with 4M87, the 11.13 Felixstowe to Trafford Park service. 28 September 2023.

More of an unusual combination this time as we see 90043 *Freightliner Coatbridge* + 57007 *Freightliner Bond* drawing to a halt at Rugby whilst working a service to Felixstowe. The Class 90 is still in service with Freightliner, currently in 'Powerhaul' livery, but stripped of its name, whilst the Class 57 is with LSL, but at present stored unserviceable at Crewe. 26 July 2006.

Three up this time as 90041+86607+86633 *Wulfruna* are seen passing through Tring with a southbound service for Felixstowe. The Class 90 is still working for Freightliner, now wearing orange and black livery, whilst 86607 has been exported to Bulgaria and 86633 was scrapped during 2013. 19 July 2003.

Up until 2023, DBC was also regularly using Class 90s on Intermodal services, but the freight company announced that these electric locos were actually costing too much to run so put a number up for sale and a few in 'warm storage', which sounds incredible in this climate-sensitive world! Anyway, this is 90020 *Collingwood* + 90040 (formerly *The Railway Mission*) passing through Stafford with 4M25, the 07.06 Mossend Euroterminal to Daventry service. 90020 is one of the examples now in warm storage, whilst 90040 was offered for sale in 2023. 13 February 2019.

Back in the early 1990s, when the Channel Tunnel was nearing completion, three examples were painted in special Continental liveries. Surprisingly, 90029 *Frachtverbindungen* retained this livery until late 2002/early 2003. It is seen here heading south hauling 92043 *Debussy*, probably bound for Wembley Yard. The Class 90 is currently in warm storage, whilst 92043 has fared rather better, now being in service with GBRF for Caledonian Sleeper Anglo-Scottish services. 4 July 2002.

Also named in conjunction with the loco in the previous shot, this is Railfreight Distribution liveried 90022 *Freightconnection* at London King's Cross on 'Thunderbird' duties, in case of any loco failures, etc. This loco was stored at Crewe as long ago as 2006 and is highly unlikely to work again. 29 July 1994.

In late 1991, the parcels sector of BR repainted 90016–90020 in its new Rail Express Systems (RES) red livery and used them mainly on Anglo-Scottish parcels/mail trains. This is 90020 *Colonel Bill Cockburn CBE TD* at London King's Cross. 29 July 1994.

This is 90024, also in Railfreight Distribution livery, at London King's Cross. Around this time, as well as the aforementioned Thunderbird duties, RFD-liveried members of the class also sometimes worked into the terminus with mail trains when the dedicated RES locos were not available. This loco is currently in warm store at Crewe. 26 May 1993.

Although the class has been mainly associated with WCML services as well as Thunderbird duties, at various times some members have been hired in to work East Coast Main Line (ECML) services, especially when Class 91 availability was quite low in the late 1990s/early 2000s. This is 90027 *Allerton T&RS Depot* awaiting departure from London King's Cross with an unidentified service for the north. *Circa* 2003.

Further down the ECML, we find a smart EWS-liveried 90040 *The Railway Mission* passing through with 1V64, the 14.09 Low Fell to Plymouth mail train. This loco was withdrawn during 2020 and in 2023 was put up for sale by DBC. 4 April 2002.

Around the end of the 1990s and beginning of the 2000s, some locos were renumbered into the 90/2 sub-class to reflect that they were fitted with different types of brake pads. These locos were often used on GNER services when they were hired in. This is 90233, approaching Doncaster with a London King's Cross to Leeds service. When used on the ECML in passenger service, they mostly worked the Leeds services as their top speed (110mph) was a bit restrictive. 19 August 2001.

As the hiring in of 90s by GNER on the ECML became a semi-permanent thing in the late 1990s, one loco, 90024, was repainted into the GNER dark blue livery to match the Mk4 coaching stock livery in use at the time. It is seen here stabled at Edinburgh Waverley. 29 February 2000.

Some Class 90s also took over haulage of the Caledonian Sleeper trains in 1998 and were painted in the First Scotrail 'Barbie' livery. This is 90021, again seen at Edinburgh Waverley. This loco was later given a unique style livery/wrap and named *Donald Malcolm* to commemorate 100 years of Malcolm Logistics, but was withdrawn from service in 2023. 1 June 2009.

To conclude this section on Class 90s, we see a few of the locos that have attended open days over the years, events that are much rarer nowadays. This is immaculate EWS-liveried 90028 on display at Crewe. This loco worked for another ten years as part of the DBC fleet, but was withdrawn in 2023. 31 May 2003.

Also immaculate in EWS livery is 90030, with a covered-up nameplate that was later revealed as *Crewe Locomotive Works*, on display at the Crewe open day. Unfortunately, this loco was withdrawn from service during January 2006. 20 May 2000.

Another smart example, again in EWS livery, is 90031 *The Railway Children Partnership – Working for Children Worldwide*. It is seen at the unlikely location of Old Oak Common Depot in West London on the Great Western Main Line. 5 August 2000.

If you thought Old Oak Common was an unusual place to see one of the class, how about these last two shots both taken at the Exeter Railfair! Looking impressive in its Railfreight Distribution livery, 90133 poses in the sunshine. This event took place in Exeter Riverside Yard, just east of Exeter St Davids station. 2 May 1994.

And finally we see Belgian-liveried 90128 *Vrachtverbinding* on display at that same Exeter Railfair. 2 May 1994.

Chapter 4

Mk3 Driving Van Trailers (DVTs)

Left: DVTs were used on many WCML/East Anglia services, so I felt it right to include a few of these for completeness. Back in the Inter-City BR days, 82123 with a service for London Euston is coming to a stand at Watford Junction to set down passengers. This example was scrapped during 2019. 27 February 1990.

Below: This is 82122 also heading south, this time through Stafford with a Glasgow Central to London Euston service. DVTs were usually on the front in the southbound direction. This was another scrapped during 2019. 22 April 1992.

Here we see 82103 in Virgin Trains livery passing Rugby with a service for London Euston. This view has changed considerably in recent years, with the remodelling of the whole station area. At the point where the train is, there is now a new island platform that has eased congestion somewhat. After being used for various adhesion tests, this vehicle was scrapped in 2020.
23 July 2004.

82109 is on the rear of a London Euston to Glasgow Central service calling at Carlisle station. These vehicles were of a very sensible and easy design that was also used as good old guards' vans for passengers' luggage, something that many new trains in use today unfortunately lack. This one has been scrapped, but the date is not known.
1 January 2004.

Very occasionally, a DVT could be found leading out of London Euston, as was the case here with 82146 passing through Watford Junction with a train for the north. A few of these vehicles were eventually withdrawn and scrapped without dates being recorded. However, this one does survive, as we will see in a while.
15 July 2001.

After withdrawal from WCML services, many DVTs saw continued use on the GEML, again operating with Class 90s after these took over from the previous Class 86s and Mk2 DVT vehicles. This is 82118 in 'one' livery, arriving at Norwich with a service from London Liverpool Street. Fortunately, this example was donated to the Crewe Heritage Centre, where it can now be seen on static display. 16 March 2007.

Whilst operating services on the GEML, the DVT was generally leading out of London. This is 82107 in National Express livery, departing from the Colchester stop with a service bound for Norwich. This one is currently stored, but it is not known where. 20 October 2011.

At the eastern end of Colchester, we see 82139 in National Express/Greater Anglia livery approaching with a London Liverpool Street to Norwich service. This is one of the lucky examples; it has been restored to Inter-City livery and is sometimes used with the preserved main line electric locos 86101/87002/90001/90002. 20 October 2011.

In the final Greater Anglia livery worn by these vehicles before being withdrawn from service, 82121 (formerly *Carlisle Cathedral*) is approaching Stratford (east London) with a London Liverpool Street to Norwich express. This vehicle is another fortunate one, as it is now preserved on the Colne Valley Railway. 29 April 2019.

It was quite unusual to see a Greater Anglia set anywhere but on the GEML. However, in tricky backlit conditions, this morning empty stock train with 82139 leading is approaching Alexandra Palace as 5E62, the 08.44 London Liverpool Street to Bounds Green T&R.S.M.D. 13 November 2018.

The only example to be painted in the revised Virgin Trains West Coast red/silver livery was 82126 (formerly *The Girls' Brigade* and *Wembley Traincare Centre*), seen here at Cow Roast, just south of Tring, with an unidentified service heading south. This vehicle has since been scrapped. 4 March 2011.

For some years, a West Coast set, complete with DVT, was used on summer Saturdays for an extra service to the West Country for holidaymakers. 82145 is on the rear of the 06.08 Preston to Paignton being hauled away from the stop at Teignmouth by 47806. The Class 47 is still in service, albeit now converted to a Class 57 as 57309 and currently used by DRS. 30 June 2001.

As mentioned earlier, 82146 has seen further use on the main line and is currently in service (though very occasionally) with DBC, working on its company train with a Class 67. With the DVT leading, it is propelled towards Chetnole on the Dorchester to Yeovil line by 67029 *Royal Diamond*, running as 1Z06, the 10.10 Weymouth to Llandrindod Wells. The scenery here is picturesque enough to evoke a heritage line. 12 May 2010.

Just after arrival at Torquay on an overcast St George's Day, this is 82146 with 1Z05, the 08.31 Ealing Broadway to Torquay. It would then proceed to work 5Z05, the 12.34 Torquay to Goodrington Sidings (Paignton), the short distance to stable overnight. 67029 *Royal Diamond* was again doing the honours at the rear. 23 April 2015.

Our final shot in this volume sees 82146 (with 67029 *Royal Diamond* propelling again), this time approaching Southampton Central with 1Z05, the 10.45 Southampton Central to London Gateway managers train. 3 June 2016.

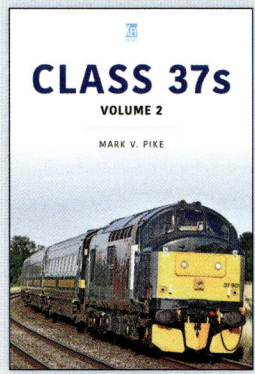
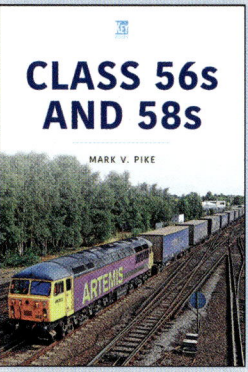
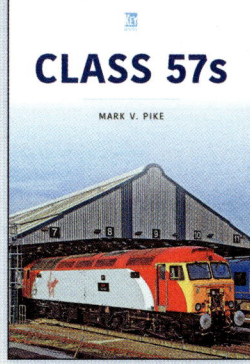
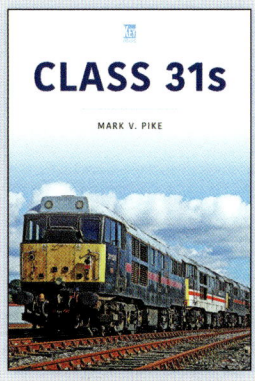
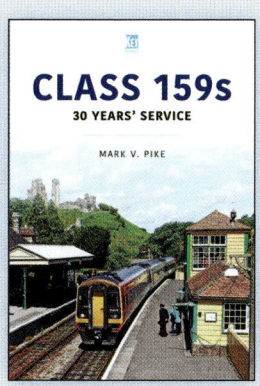
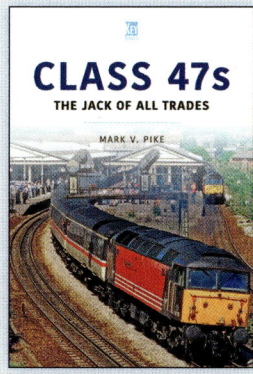